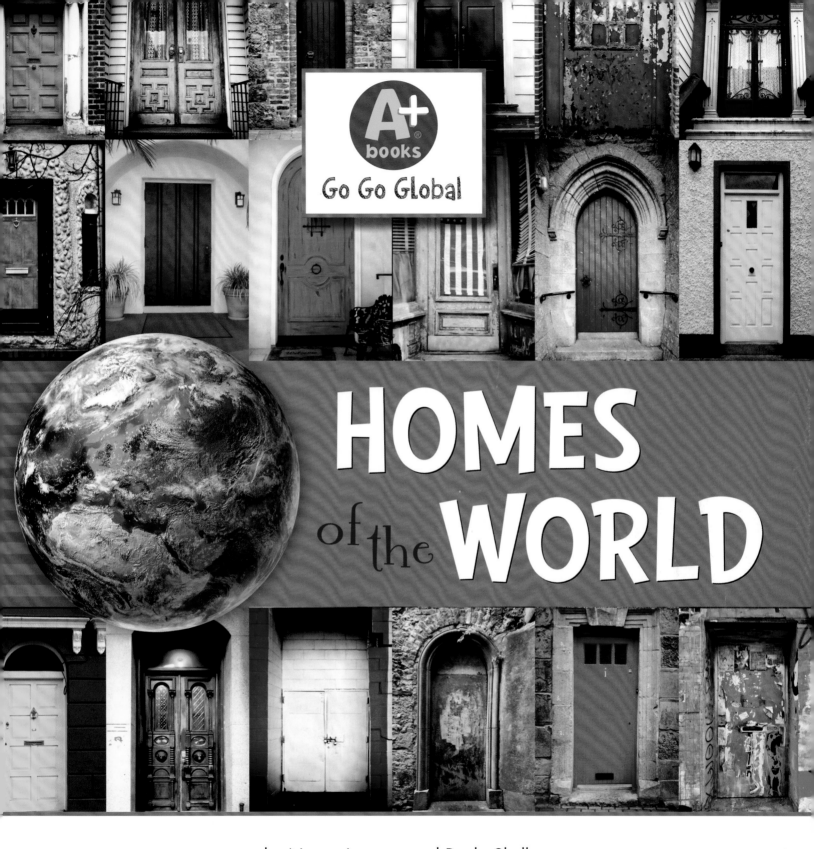

A+ books

Go Go Global

HOMES of the WORLD

by Nancy Loewen and Paula Skelley

CAPSTONE PRESS
a capstone imprint

China

South Africa

Around the **world,**

up high

and

low,

2

Greece

white,

Honduras

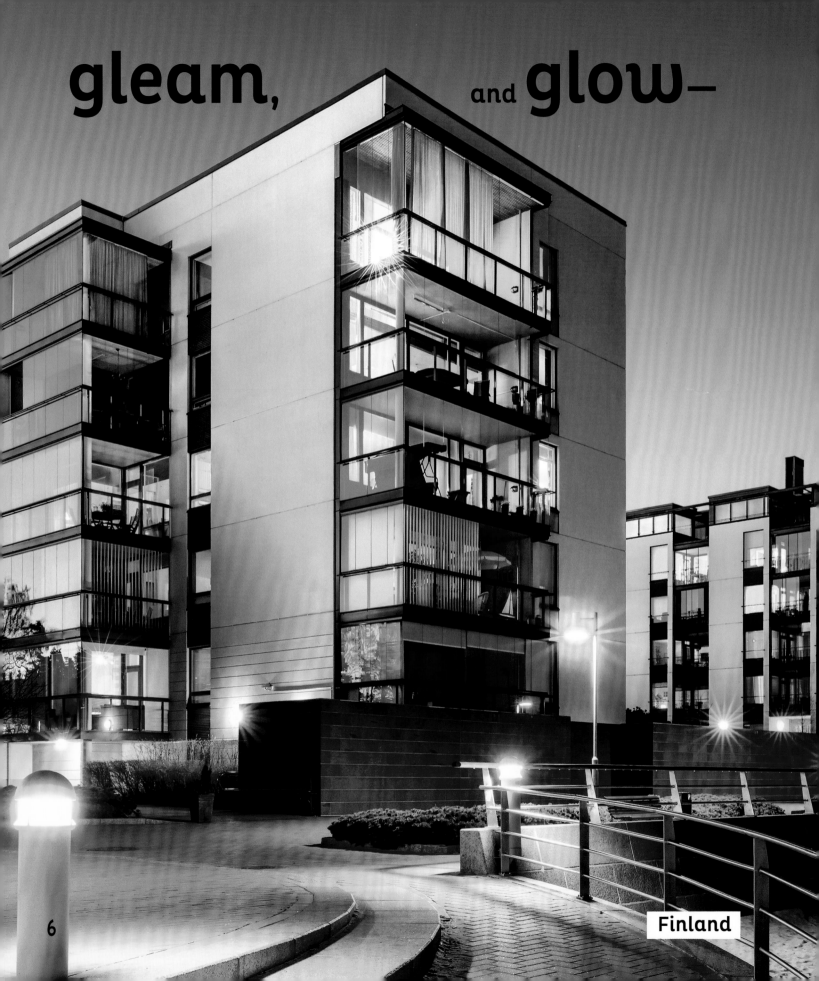

gleam, and glow–

Finland

Denmark

homes are where
we **live** and **grow**.

From **sunbaked clay**

United States

to **solid stones,**

England

many **materials** make up our **homes.**

Bricks are strong.

Ghana

Thatch

keeps us **dry**.

Australia

Logs and mud

Canada

shelter **people** inside.

Kenya

Some **homes**

are made to **share**–

England

all in a **row**

or high in the air!

China

Other **homes** are made for a **few**—

Suriname

England

though **neighbors** are certainly **welcome** too.

17

United States

Homes are puzzles with shapes you know:

circles,

squares,

Mongolia

Japan

triangles ...

South Africa

Now here's a
challenge,
you'll agree:
Count up all the
rectangles!

21

Homes on water?

Italy

Sure!

Homes on homes?

Netherlands

Why not?

On sandy dunes

Morocco

and **mountaintops** ...

Greenland

homes on lots of **great spots!**

Whether it's old

Brazil

Iran

or whether it's **new,**

Australia

a **home** is **a special place**— for **YOU**.

United States

Colombia

Greenland

Canada

**NORTH
AMERICA**

United
States

Honduras

Colombia

Suriname

**SOUTH
AMERICA**

Brazil

Finland

Denmark

England
Netherlands

EUROPE

Italy

Greece

Iran

Morocco

AFRICA

Ghana

Kenya

South
Africa

ANTARCTICA

Mongolia

ASIA

China

Japan

AUSTRALIA

Australia

GLOSSARY

dune—a hill or ridge of sand piled up by the wind

gleam—a small bright light

location—the place where something is

material—what something is made of or used for

shelter—to cover and keep safe

thatch—straw, reeds, or similar material that is used to cover a roof

CRITICAL THINKING USING THE COMMON CORE

1. What do all of the homes in this book have in common? (Key Ideas and Details)

2. Name four materials used to build homes. (Key Ideas and Details)

3. Which homes in this book are most unlike your home? How are they different? (Integration of Knowledge and Ideas)

A+ Books are published by Capstone Press,
1710 Roe Crest Drive, North Mankato, Minnesota 56003
www.capstonepub.com

Library of Congress Cataloging-in-Publication Data
Cataloging-in-publication information is on file with the Library of Congress.
ISBN 978-1-4914-3919-7 (library binding)
ISBN 978-1-4914-3930-2 (paperback)
ISBN 978-1-4914-3940-1 (eBook PDF)

Editorial Credits
Jill Kalz, editor; Juliette Peters, designer; Tracy Cummins, media researcher; Tori Abraham, production specialist

Photo Credits
Dreamstime: Lars Christensen, 7, Melonstone, 17, Thomas Lozinski, 4; iStockphoto Inc: Andrew Rich/Rich Vintage Photography, 27 Bottom, BartCo, 16, hadynyah, 19 Top, ManoAfrica, 2 Bottom, oversnap, 25 Top; Shutterstock: 135pixels, 9, alenvl, Cover TL, alysta, 14, Andresr, 29, Anton_Ivanov, 11, astudio, 24, Birute Vijeikiene, 13, Charmaine A Harvey, 20, Ekaterina Kamenetsky, 10, elvistudio, 28, GuoZhongHua, 15, Hung Chung Chih, Cover TR, Hurst Photo, 3, KennStilger47, 18, Kwiatek7, Cover BR, Kzenon, 2 Top, leocalvett, Cover, 1, (globe), littleny, 1, Oleksiy Mark, 6, Panos Karas, 5, Pics-xl 23, Publio Furbino 26 Top, Scott Prokop, 12, Shaiith, 22, Stawek, 30, Volodymyr Kyrylyuk, Cover Back, Workait Sirijinda, 19 Bottom, Yauhen Novikau, 26 Bottom, ZRyzner, Cover BL, zstock, 27 Top; Thinkstock: Karen H. Johnson, 8.

READ MORE

Benjamin, Tina. *Where I Live.* Inside My World. New York: Gareth Stevens Publishing, 2015.

Cane, Ella. *Homes in My World.* My World. North Mankato, Minn.: Capstone Press, 2014.

Smith, Siân. *Homes That Move.* Where We Live. Chicago: Heinemann Library, 2014.

INTERNET SITES

FactHound offers a safe, fun way to find Internet sites related to this book. All of the sites on FactHound have been researched by our staff.

Here's all you do:
Visit *www.facthound.com*
Type in this code:
9781491439197

 Check out projects, games and lots more at **www.capstonekids.com**

Printed in China.
032015   008864WMF15